How to Thrive in a ~~~~

By Gene Roncone

ABOUT THE AUTHOR

Gene Roncone has a passion to help local churches experience healthy pastoral transitions. He presently leads the Rocky Mountain Ministry Network where he provides support, resourcing, and training for nearly 170 churches and 600 ministers serving over 44,000 constituents in Colorado and Utah. Gene is the author of Rise Up, the most researched, comprehensive, and practical reference work on pastoral transitions available. He has also authored several books including, *Explore the Call*, *Isolation in Ministry*, *Prevailing Over Impossibility*, and *A Season for Legacy*. He enjoys reading and writing in the Colorado wilderness and spending time with his wife, Rhonda, and their adult children and their grandchildren. You can contact Gene through www.generoncone.org.

Dedicated to the faithful men and women who served as deacons during my tenure at Highpoint Church. We bled, cried, laughed, and led together as God moved in miraculous ways. I am a better man, pastor, and leader because of you.

Table of Contents

May the LORD, the God who gives breath to all living things, appoint someone over this community to go out and come in before them, one who will lead them out and bring them in, so the LORD'S people will not be like sheep without a shepherd.
Numbers 27:16-17 NIV

Introduction

We live in a day of glamorized activism, unyielding opinions, and fierce individualism. Even in the church, we celebrate our differences much more than what we have in common. However, a verse in the Old Testament reminds God's people of the infinite potential of unified focus:

> *All the people assembled with a unified purpose...*
> Nehemiah 8:1 (NLT)

There are few occasions where unity of purpose is needed more than when a church is experiencing a pastoral transition. When unity is accompanied by focus and commitment, there is very little God's people cannot accomplish.

That is why this book was written. It was designed to be your personal survival guide for your own pastoral transition. It is a powerful tool that can help you rise above the discouragement so often associated with pastoral transitions and build your faith in the fact that God has a plan for you and your church.

By reading it and using the reflection questions at the end of each chapter, you will have the potential to become a positive influence in your church. You will learn the following four skills to thrive and flourish in this season of change:

- How to grow spiritually during a pastoral transition.
- How to love, support, and care for your new pastor.
- How to embrace God's new thing (Isaiah 43:19).
- How to pray for every stage and person involved in your pastoral transition.

You may also find useful my entire family of pastoral transition resources called *Rise Up* at www.generoncone.org/riseup.[1] This book and these resources were created to help you not only survive this transition but also to thrive in it!

Gene Roncone
Aurora, Colorado

1. God's Word and Leadership Transitions

Pastoral transitions are not inconvenient interruptions that must be painfully endured. As a matter of fact, one of the biggest mistakes you can make is to think that this transition has little to do with you. Pastoral transitions are strategic times that God uses to grow you spiritually.

As a matter of fact, there is something in your spiritual life that you need but can only experience on the other side of this transition. As someone who specializes in pastoral transitions, I have found that one of the most disappointing realities is how few believers really understand the biblical purpose of leadership changes. If you do not, you may end up weaker on the other side of this change rather than stronger. Some see them as an interruption to be endured while others become detoured by the pitfalls so common in change. A few allow their selfishness to blind them from God's will and others even fall off the radar.

However, the fact of the matter is that God has something so important to your future that you can only experience it on the other side of change. As strange as it may sound, this transition will be one of the biggest growth opportunities you will have in your walk with God, but you must be ready to embrace it and grow.

Missing the growth opportunities of leadership transitions is not a new pitfall. The Corinthian church in the New Testament made this mistake more than once while experiencing leadership changes in their own church. The sad thing is they should have and could have done better.

The church in Corinth was blessed with some of the finest leadership the early church had to offer. Their pastoral roster could have been considered the "dream team" of New Testament leadership. They sat under the ministry of Paul, the driven, strategic, and theological apostle of soaring faith. He was a powerful leader who wrote two-thirds of the New Testament. In addition, they also sat under the ministry of Peter. Imagine being mentored by a dynamic, inspiring, and down-to-earth disciple who knew Jesus intimately! As if that were not enough, the Bible tells us that Apollos also ministered in Corinth. We do not know much about him except that he was a silver-tongued orator who spoke with the eloquence of a trial attorney. Apollos was so persuasive that Jewish zealots came to confess Christ as their savior.

What a deep leadership bench! You would think this legacy of leadership would have resulted in an incredibly mature and effective church. Unfortunately, it did not. As a matter of fact, the Apostle Paul had to give the Corinthians some firm correction regarding their perspective of leadership transitions.

> *[10] I appeal to you, brothers and sisters, in the name of our Lord Jesus Christ, that all of you agree with one another in what you say and that there be no divisions among you, but that you be perfectly united in mind and thought. [11] My brothers and sisters, some from Chloe's household have informed me that there are quarrels among you. [12] What I mean is this: One of you says, "I follow Paul"; another, "I follow Apollos"; another, "I follow Cephas"; still another, "I follow Christ." [13] Is Christ divided? Was Paul crucified for you? Were you baptized in the name of Paul? [14] I thank God that I did not baptize any of you except Crispus and Gaius, [15] so no one can say that you were baptized in my name. [16] (Yes, I also baptized the household of Stephanas; beyond that, I don't remember if I baptized anyone else.) [17] For Christ did not send me to baptize, but to*

preach the gospel—not with wisdom and eloquence, lest the cross of Christ be emptied of its power (1 Corinthians 1:10-17 NIV).

¹Brothers and sisters, I could not address you as people who live by the Spirit but as people who are still worldly—mere infants in Christ. ²I gave you milk, not solid food, for you were not yet ready for it. Indeed, you are still not ready. ³You are still worldly. For since there is jealousy and quarreling among you, are you not worldly? Are you not acting like mere humans? ⁴For when one says, "I follow Paul," and another, "I follow Apollos," are you not mere human beings? ⁵What, after all, is Apollos? And what is Paul? Only servants, through whom you came to believe—as the Lord has assigned to each his task. ⁶I planted the seed, Apollos watered it, but God has been making it grow. ⁷So neither the one who plants nor the one who waters is anything, but only God, who makes things grow. ⁸The one who plants and the one who waters have one purpose, and they will each be rewarded according to their own labor. ⁹For we are co-workers in God's service; you are God's field, God's building (1 Corinthians 3:1-9 NIV).

What can we learn from Paul's advice about how to thrive during a pastoral transition? Let's find out.

2. Stay United as a Church

If you are going to experience spiritual growth through this pastoral transition, you must stay unified as a church. The Corinthians were divided over what kind of spiritual leader they preferred, and Paul said to them: *I appeal to you, brothers and sisters, in the name of our Lord Jesus Christ, that all of you agree with one another in what you say and that there be no divisions among you, but that you be perfectly united in mind and thought* (1 Corinthians 1:10 NIV). Instead of being united, the Corinthians were divided by many things when it came to spiritual leaders in their lives. The enemy thrives in environments charged with division, competing interests, and ego. If you want to grow through this transition, you and your church must be committed to preserving unity.

They were divided by their personal preferences. This happens when we allow our preferences to become more important than our principles. There is a big difference between these two things. Principles are undisputable truths that are nonnegotiable—things like the deity of Jesus Christ, the way of salvation, the Trinity, holiness, and other doctrinal beliefs. We should fight for principles because they are absolute truths and biblical doctrines that do not change. However, preferences are based on our personal desires, tastes, and styles. Preferences are things like worship, preaching, or leadership styles we personally prefer. The Corinthians allowed their preferences of leadership style, ministry models, preaching, and temperaments to divide them. God is going to bring many different spiritual leaders in and out of your life. Each will have things you like about them and things you do not. Each leader will gravitate towards different ministries, expressions of worship, and strategies. If you are not careful in this pastoral transition, you can make the mistake of assuming that what you prefer is as important as the biblical principles you embrace.

There is one other important thing to remember about preferences if you want to stay united. The right of preference should be left to those who are entrusted with the responsibilities associated with that area. If a committee is appointed to select the kind of chairs your church will buy, then let them choose the chairs and colors. They have been given the right of preference. In the same way, if your church bylaws charge your board or pastoral search committee with the job of screening potential candidates, then they have the right of preference. Division happens when we try to pry the right of preference out of the hands of those who are entrusted with it.

They were divided by selfishness. The Corinthians were also looking at their own needs through the lens of self rather than through the lens of what God wanted to do in their community of faith. That is why Paul confronted them saying, *I could not address you as people who live by the Spirit but as people who are still worldly—mere infants in Christ...You are still worldly. For since there is jealousy and quarreling among you, are you not worldly?* (1 Corinthians 3:1,3 NIV).

If you are like I am, you have personal needs that shape what you want, admire, and support. However, do not allow your personal needs to turn you into a topical lobbyist or spiritual activist during this pastoral transition. It is not about you or your needs so much as it is about where God wants to take your church and His vision of the future. To assume your needs are the same as God's in this transition would be a mistake.

They were divided by unhealthy loyalties. Paul challenged them with the fact that they were more loyal to previous leaders and personality styles than they were to Christ. He called them out saying: *What I mean is this: One of you says, "I follow Paul"; another, "I follow Apollos"; another, "I follow Cephas"; still another, "I follow Christ." Is Christ divided? Was Paul crucified for you? Were you baptized in the name of Paul?* (1 Corinthians 1:12-13 NIV).

If you look at the different spiritual leaders God sent to Corinth, they could not have been more diverse. Paul was the typical "Type A" personality whose strategic planning, soaring faith, and daunting courage conquered much of the New Testament world. On the other hand, Apollos may have been the greatest preacher of the New Testament period. He was an orator whose preaching resembled the closing arguments of a skilled trial attorney. Then there was Peter or, as Paul referred to him, Cephas. Peter was the passionate, impulsive, blue-collar guy who was the working man's hero. I think he would have been the kind of pastor who liked to hunt, fish, and go to ball games with his people. And who could forget the fourth leader Paul mentioned: Jesus, our model of perfection.

The Corinthians could not be unified because they were divided by their personal preferences, needs, and loyalties. As a result, they were so overly committed to their past that they could not embrace God's future.

Making It Real

Following are a few questions to discuss or reflect upon:
*   What are some modern examples of how you might elevate a personal preference to the level of a principle?

- In what ways might your church become divided by an unhealthy reliance upon the personality or giftings of a pastor?
- How might an unhealthy attachment or dependence upon a pastor cause you to miss God-sized opportunities in the present and future?

3. Decide Whom You Are Following

Another thing you must do to grow through this transition is to decide whom you are following. The Corinthians had to make the same decision. Were they committed to a man or to Christ? That is what Paul was driving at when he asked, *Is Christ divided? Was Paul crucified for you? Were you baptized in the name of Paul?* (1 Corinthians 1:13 NIV).

It is common for each of us to become endeared to the people who lead us spiritually. This kind of spiritual bonding is healthy; but what is not healthy is when our commitment to unity, our church, and spiritual passion becomes dependent upon the personality of a pastor.

Paul rocks their world, questions their spiritual maturity, and challenges them to consider whom they are really following. He reminds them that it is Christ and not their spiritual leaders whom they must be focused upon. Paul, Apollos, and Peter did not die on a cross for them. Furthermore, they were not baptized in the name of their previous pastors. God sends different spiritual leaders in and out of our lives, but it is Christ and Christ alone we must follow.

After pastoring for 24 years and serving as a faith-based executive for another 9, I have found that few things reveal a person's true dedication to Christ as a pastoral transition. Unfortunately, it is when a church is without a pastor that you see what really motivates people. Let me challenge you to consider that it is Christ and not some romanticized version of the past or a pastor whom you are following. Remember that when you are deciding whether you will:

- Be faithful to church services during the transition.
- Remain consistent in giving your tithes and offerings.
- Continue volunteering to help and fill in gaps during this season when your church needs you.
- Continue praying for the search committee, the board, and the church during this critical time.

When this search is over and you look back upon your actions, whom will they show you were following—Christ or man?

Making It Real

Following are a few questions to discuss or reflect upon:
- What might be some indications that you are following a person rather than Christ?
- Statistics show that many churches experience a slight decline in attendance, giving, volunteerism, and church engagement during a pastoral transition. What does Paul's teaching to the Corinthians say about the reason for these trends?

4. Embrace Spiritual Maturity

This transition is going to expose the level of your spiritual maturity. Growing through it will require you to make important spiritual decisions each day. This is another area in which the Corinthians missed the mark. They thought of themselves as spiritually mature people, but Paul claimed their behavior only proved they were childish. He challenged them saying, *I could not address you as people who live by the Spirit but as people who are still worldly—mere infants in Christ. I gave you milk, not solid food, for you were not yet ready for it. Indeed, you are still not ready* (1 Corinthians 3:1-2 NIV).

By calling out the immaturity of the Corinthians in their own leadership transitions, Paul reveals a few characteristics of spiritual maturity during these times.

Maturity understands that pastoral transitions are spiritual in nature. Paul warned the Corinthians that they were viewing spiritual leadership through a worldly lens, not a spiritual one. Maturity will require you to live by the Spirit. Finding the person God has already chosen to be your pastor is not a corporate hiring practice but a spiritual process. That process requires prayer, discernment, submission, and a sensitivity to the Holy Spirit, and God's will.

If you are a businessperson, there can be a temptation to lean on secular hiring methods, your business background, or Human Resource policies. After all, that is how you have been doing it for years; and you have established steps, forms, and HR processes that have worked. I remember a meeting I was in and a board member who was a high-level administrator brought in a huge three-ring binder from his

HR Department. He naively thought it should serve as a guide for the church board. However, finding the person God has already called to lead your church is much different for many reasons. Do not get me wrong; there are some corporate skills that are transferable and even helpful to a point, but sooner or later they take you down the wrong path or hinder progress. Why? Four reasons:

First, the hiring skills most businesspeople have learned were created in the vacuum of a for-profit environment. The criteria that drove those policies and the values behind them were profitability, results, competitive marketing, and employment laws that do not recognize spiritual priorities, biblical authority, or an eternal perspective. It is like taking the business plan of a computer factory and superimposing it over that of a dairy farm.

Second, identifying whom God has called to pastor your church is more about character than accomplishment. It is not that the corporate world is uninterested in character. They are to a point, but their view of character is jaded and confined either to the workplace or its impact upon the company's brand or reputation. It is linear while the spiritual process of choosing a pastor is multidimensional.

Third, corporate hiring practices are guided by changing laws and HR "wokeness" rather than the Bible's absolute truths. In the corporate world, something can be legal but biblically unethical. Other times some practices can be forbidden in the business world but preferred spiritually. For example, it is legal for a CEO to hire a prostitute in Las Vegas, buy or sell marijuana, or even be shrewd when negotiating contracts. These things can be considered "normal" in the corporate world but unacceptable for believers. Calling every member to prayer and fasting is critical in the church but considered inappropriate and intrusive at work.

Fourth, corporate hiring methods do not intentionally seek or recognize the supernatural. They are intentionally designed to be predicable, measurable, and prescribed. However, pastoral engagement is very much dependent upon the supernatural, and unexplainable. By its very nature, pastoral selections may not always mirror our own desires. For example, when the prophet Samuel was creating his short list of candidates to be anointed as the new king of Israel, he almost missed God's will. Why? Because he looked at appearance and failed to ask God. As a result, he overlooked the most divinely qualified candidate and picked a man named Eliab. God had to shake an anointed prophet out of spiritual slumber and say, *Do not look on his appearance or on the height of his stature, because I have rejected him. For the* LORD *sees not as man sees: man looks on the outward appearance, but the* LORD *looks on the heart* (1 Samuel 16:7 ESV).

Who was the candidate Samuel's logical methodology missed? David, the man after God's own heart who would become one of the nation's greatest kings. In this case, the search committee's infatuation with optics and qualifications almost caused them to miss God's will! Corporate hiring methods can be helpful to a point; but in the end, they are like a 7-foot ladder against a 30-foot wall. They just fall short of what the spiritual task requires.

Maturity seeks wisdom, not just knowledge. Paul told the Corinthians they were "mere infants" who were still on milk and not ready for solid food. He was talking about the gap that can exists between spiritual knowledge and spiritual wisdom. The primary difference between those two words is that wisdom involves a perspective and ability to make sound decisions. Knowledge is simply knowing on the linear plane of data and facts. Anyone can become knowledgeable about a subject by reading, researching, and memorizing details. However, wisdom requires us to operate in a three-dimensional realm where we must determine which facts are relevant at the right time and place as well as how they should be applied. In very much the same way, your pastoral transition will require knowledge of best practices plus spiritual wisdom. For the church board, it will relate to the pastoral search process. For you, it will be required in how you steward your words, actions, priorities, opinions, finances, and self-control.

Maturity values unity over division. Paul called out what he described as "jealousy and quarreling" that existed among the Corinthians. Let me remind you that this pastoral search will find your weaknesses. It will bring out the best and the worst among you and other members of your church. There will be many opportunities for you to choose between gossip or encouragement, fear or faith, control or surrender, activism or cooperation, unity or division as well as patience or irritation. Protecting the ministries of candidates, due diligence and avoiding the politicization of the process will require strict confidentiality by your search committee. Your ability to trust and stay united without knowledge of details will be tested.

Paul later told the Corinthians that God allows division to show the body of Christ who is spiritually mature: *There must be factions among you in order that those who are genuine among you may be recognized* (1 Corinthians 11:19 ESV). The word "genuine" in this context also means mature. May I encourage you to be among those who are spiritually and emotionally mature during this search process. A mature believer makes the following five decisions each day during a pastoral transition:

- I choose to see this transition through a spiritual perspective rather than a worldly one.

- I choose to be the voice of reason when fear and uncertainty seem to prevail.
- I choose to move on with the future that God has for me.
- I choose to be a partner in unity rather than a participant of discord.
- I choose to surrender to God's will rather than a codependency on man.

Making It Real

Following are a few questions to discuss or reflect upon:
- Think about the different stages involved in a pastoral search process. How might you think or act immaturely in these various stages?
- What are examples of mature ways you can respond to the confidential nature by which a pastoral search must be carried out?
- What are examples of mature ways you can support your board as they seek God's will, navigate this process, and lead in this transition?
- What are examples of mature ways you can respond to opportunities to gossip, register criticism, or act upon your fleshly fears?
- What are examples of mature ways you can process your own preferences regarding who or what the next pastor should be and do?
- What are examples of mature ways you can respond to the everyday needs of your church ministries, finances, and Sunday services?

5. Remember Your Source

Every pastoral transition is an opportunity to rediscover God as your true source of direction, wisdom, and strength. This is what the Corinthians forgot and what Paul reminded them about:

> *³…Are you not acting like mere humans? ⁴For when one says, "I follow Paul," and another, "I follow Apollos," are you not mere human beings? ⁵What, after all, is Apollos? And what is Paul? Only servants, through whom you came to believe— as the Lord has assigned to each his task. ⁶I planted the seed, Apollos watered it, but God has been making it grow. ⁷So neither the one who plants nor the one who waters is anything, but only God, who makes things grow. ⁸The one who plants and the one who waters have one purpose, and they will each be rewarded according to their own labor* (1 Corinthians 3:3-8 NIV).

There are three powerful principles in this passage you must remember if you want to thrive in this pastoral transition.

First, pastors are conduits, not the source of spiritual growth. Paul asks the question, *What, after all, is Apollos? And what is Paul? Only servants, through whom you came to believe* (1 Corinthians 3:5 NIV). The key to understanding what is happening in a pastoral transition is locked up in the word "through" which means "by way of," "channel," or "pipeline." There is a difference between the water you need to survive and the pipes from which that water flows. In other words, the spiritual leaders God brings in and out of your life are only the conduits by which God brings spiritual sustenance to your spirit. However, they are not the source. You have probably had pastors with whom you have personally connected with in your life, but those men and women are not the water! They are the pipeline by which your heavenly Father blesses you. The conduit may change, but the source does not.

Second, God has ordained this season in your life. You and others may have different theories about how and why this leadership transition has occurred, but Paul assures us that God is orchestrating events to take both you and your church to a new level the future will require. Paul reminds the Corinthians of this fact with penetrating questions: *What, after all, is Apollos? And what is Paul? Only servants, through whom you came to believe—as the Lord has assigned to each his task. I planted the seed, Apollos watered it, but God has been making it grow* (1 Corinthians 3:5-6 NIV).

God uses different spiritual leaders in your life to grow your faith. Some till the soil and others fertilize. One plants the seeds of the season and another waters. Some prune and cut off the dead and decaying wood while others bring new growth. Although each has a differing task, God has called and ordained them to serve a unique purpose in your life.

Third, God is using this transition to grow you. Paul makes it clear that every leadership transition in your life has a purpose—spiritual growth: *God has been making it grow. So neither the one who plants nor the one who waters is anything, but only God, who makes things grow. God has been making it grow* (1 Corinthians 3:6-7 NIV).

If God is leading this transition as Paul said, then He has a plan. This transition is going to bring something to your life that you cannot and would not be able to access without it. That means God, not inconvenient change, is at the helm of your present. What can be more exciting than that?

Making It Real

Following are a few questions to discuss or reflect upon:

- What might an unhealthy dependence upon a pastor reveal about your spiritual maturity and surrender to Christ?
- What are a few practical ways you can keep your eyes on Christ in your pastoral transition?

6. Let God Grow You

If you are going to flourish in this pastoral transition, then you must cooperate with God and allow Him to grow you. Some believers hinder God from growing them by competing with Him, getting in the way, and resisting the new things He is trying to do. That is why Paul reminded the Corinthians to get out of the way and allow God to grow them: *For we are co-workers in God's service; you are God's field, God's building* (1 Corinthians 3:9 NIV).

Paul used three analogies to describe what God is doing right now in your life. He calls you God's co-worker, God's field, and God's building. All three of these comparisons can be a source of confidence for you through this transition.

Let God grow you by cooperating with Him. I love that Paul describes us as co-workers with God. That means change is not happening to us; it is happening with us. However, God needs your cooperation, collaboration, and team spirit. He needs your surrender, trust, and sincere effort to make this a smooth and effective transition. If you resist and compete with God, then you will miss the future the present is preparing you to face.

Let God grow you by surrendering your heart. The second thing Paul says is that we are God's field. Your heart is a field that God is working to make fruitful. There are several stages of farming that give us a hint as to what God is asking of you during this time.

The first stage of farming is tilling, plowing, and preparing the soil. That means God is going to stir things up to make the soil of your heart ready to receive the seeds of the new thing He is going to do.

The second stage is planting and sowing seeds. In other words, He is going to entrust you with small seeds that have the potential to grow a greater harvest. These seeds may seem unimpressive at the front end of this transition, but your job is to let them grow and help nurture them.

The third stage of farming is fertilizing the soil so the seeds get the right nutrients and can flourish. This sounds a lot better than it smells because fertilizer is a fancy way of saying manure. No one likes manure because it is messy, smelly, and unpleasant; but Proverbs 14:4 says it best: *Without oxen a stable stays clean, but you need a strong ox for a large harvest* (NLT). Therefore, if you want your church to have a large harvest, you must be willing to be around manure, get your hands dirty, and tolerate some poo.

The fourth stage of farming is irrigation. This happens when God waters you and your church to increase your harvest potential. A good farmer waters the crop in small consistent amounts, not all at once. That means God's most important blessing will come in small but consistent ways. I think that is why Zechariah 4:10 encourages us not to despise the day of "small things".

The last stage is harvesting and storage. This is the most exciting part because this is when growth produces more growth. If you are God's field, then you need to surrender your life, preferences, and church to allow God to cultivate your heart. Are you willing to do that? I hope so.

Let God grow you by trusting His plan. The third analogy Paul compares you to is a building. That means God is not winging it or shooting from the hip. He is working from a detailed blueprint and building you and your church into something grand. There will be times in the next few months or even years following your pastoral transition that things might not make sense. You may even have trouble connecting the dots, but you must trust the Divine Architect. He has drafted a set of detailed blueprints for you and your church, and they are amazing!

Making It Real

Following are a few questions to discuss or reflect upon:
- Brainstorm and come up with a list of areas in which you and other members of your church must cooperate with God to grow spiritually in this season of development.
- What might tilling, fertilizing, tending, pruning, and growing look like in this process?
- How does it make you feel hearing that leadership transitions are part of God's master plan for your life?

7. Something Is Changing, and It Is Not Good

I feel the ground moving beneath me! Like shifting tectonic plates, something is changing in the church and it is not good. Pastors are leaving the ministry, suffering from depression, and even taking their own lives in record numbers. Author Richard Clinton claims that 70 percent of those who enter the ministry will not retire from it.[2] Chuck Hannaford, a clinical psychologist who consults for the Southern Baptist Convention, said he believes the rate of pastoral suicides has increased during his 30 years of practice and he expects the number will continue to rise.[3]

We are experiencing a national crisis among our ministers that cannot be ignored. God's people are becoming impossible to please, and cultural forces have made pastoring harder than ever. Some churches are burning through pastors like disposable cups. These churches usually lack a culture of encouragement and tolerate an abusive minority that resents the thought that pastors are spiritual gifts to be supported, protected, and honored. But, pastors are to be honored not because they are more important than others but because they are more critical to the church's mission (1 Corinthians 12:21-24).

The church may struggle with this concept, but NASA does not. NASA understands strategic importance and critical exposure. For example, not all the exterior tiles of the Space Shuttle are the same. They vary in cost, thickness, size, and materials. The tiles on the belly of the Shuttle require special attention because they are exposed to temperatures up to 2,300 degrees Fahrenheit during reentry. That is why they are given a special protective coating of black glass. More resources are also used to design tiles that provide protection to areas that are vulnerable to damage from space debris. Why? Because if one of those tiles were to be compromised under the heat of reentry, the entire Shuttle, crew, and mission could be lost. These tiles are prioritized because of their strategic purpose—not because of their individual value.

The same thing is true spiritually. Our enemy, the devil, is smart. He knows if he can take out your pastor, he can do more harm to the church than attacking a random member. That is why your pastor faces more extreme and strategically focused attacks from the enemy on his body, soul, mind, family, marriage, and finances.

Some resent the idea that pastors should receive special honor, appreciation, or recognition. They argue that everyone in the body is equally important. Although true, this lethal logic ignores a biblical understanding of spiritual warfare. Paul reminded us of this: *For our struggle is not against flesh and blood, but against the rulers, against the authorities, against the powers of this dark world and against the spiritual forces of evil in the heavenly realms* (Ephesians 6:12 NIV).

Pastors need specialized care because they face more heat—not because they are more important than others. Therefore, in the next few chapters, I want to talk about why and how to love and care for your new pastor. I have selected Hebrews 13:17 from several different translations to help you see how different scholars have tried to interpret and illuminate the meaning of this verse.

> *Have confidence in your leaders and submit to their authority, because they keep watch over you as those who must give an account. Do this so that their work will be a joy, not a burden, for that would be of no benefit to you* (NIV).

Obey your leaders and submit to them, for they are keeping watch over your souls, as those who will have to give an account. Let them do this with joy and not with groaning, for that would be of no advantage to you (ESV).

Listen to your leaders and submit to their authority over the community, for they are on constant watch to protect your souls and someday they must give account. Give them reason to be joyful and not to regret their duty, for that will be of no good to you (VOICE).

Be responsive to your pastoral leaders. Listen to their counsel. They are alert to the condition of your lives and work under the strict supervision of God. Contribute to the joy of their leadership, not its drudgery. Why would you want to make things harder for them? (MSG).

Believe it or not, God has already chosen your next pastor; but until He reveals His will to your church, you can start preparing to support them now.

Making It Real

Following are a few questions to discuss or reflect upon:

- As politics, race relations, and cultural conflicts become uglier, do you see that negativity spilling over into the church? If so, how?
- We live in a culture that employs activism, criticism, and personal attacks instead of biblical principles of conflict resolution to get the attention of our leaders. Why are these methods infiltrating the church?
- Were you surprised to learn that depression, discouragement, and suicide among pastors is on the rise? What might God's people be doing to contribute to that trend?

8. Why Support Your Pastor

Just as NASA predetermined to provide support for strategic assets so must you on a spiritual level. Following are a few reasons why.

You should support your pastor because they are a gift from God to the church. Paul wrote: *Christ himself gave the apostles, the prophets, the evangelists, the pastors and teachers, to equip his people for works of service, so that the body of Christ may be built up* (Ephesians 4:11-12 NIV).

That is a powerful thought to ponder. A pastor is not a hireling, outsider, or employee. A pastor is a gift that "Christ himself" gave, provided, and entrusted to your church.

You should support your pastor because they keep watch over your soul. Hebrews encourages us to support our pastors because of the nature of their spiritual work in our lives. *Obey your leaders and submit to them, for they are keeping watch over your souls, as those who will have to give an account. Let them do this with joy and not with groaning, for that would be of no advantage to you* (Hebrews 13:17 ESV).

How does a pastor keep watch over your soul? They feed, nurture, and build up your spirit. They keep you going and, like a compass, point you to our spiritual "true north". They study to teach you God's Word and mature your faith. They guard against theological error, spiritual assault, and division. They pray for you when you are sick, discouraged, or suffering. They keep watch over your soul with the diligence of a Secret Service agent.

I pastored for 24 years before serving in my present capacity. To be honest, I have at times struggled with my spiritual gift mix. It seemed boring and lacked any of the power gifts like healing, prophecy, or miracles. My spiritual gifts are teaching, leadership, administration, and discernment. Not an impressive mix, right? But the older I get, the more my gift of discernment seems to develop and sharpen. On one occasion I was walking through the children's wing of my church and was suddenly overcome with a keen awareness of the presence of evil when a young man walked by me. I did a quick turnabout and started following the person until he left the children's wing and walked out of the building. I later informed a member of our security team to keep an eye on him. This team member worked at the local Air Force base with a small Secret Service unit. He asked me to give him the young man's name, age, and address. As it turned out, he had a history of torturing animals and sexually abusing minors. Needless to say, he never stepped foot in our children's area again. It was another reminder to me of the importance of the gift of pastoring, discernment, and watching over the souls of others.

You should support your pastor because it is to your benefit to do so. Unfortunately, there are a few Christians who prefer to have a competitive relationship with their pastor. Whether it is at work, home, or church, they take pleasure in challenging, questioning, and criticizing authority figures in their life. They never seem to miss an opportunity to take their spiritual leaders down a notch or two. Some even believe this is their role in the church. However, the book of Hebrews teaches us that this is more harmful to them than it is to their pastor. Making your pastor's job harder, more unpleasant, and burdensome is actually a disadvantage to you! As a matter of fact, Hebrews presents the two extremes of pastoral service as joy and drudgery and says you and I have a biblical obligation to use our influence to make our pastor's work pleasant. Or you can turn that principal around and say a happy, joyful, and encouraged pastor translates into a blessing to you!

Making It Real

Following are a few questions to discuss or reflect upon:

- Scripture teaches us that pastors are God's gift to the church (Ephesians 4:11-12). What does the fact that pastors are God's gift to us say about how we should understand their purpose?
- Have you ever given a gift to someone who did not appreciate or respect it? How did it make you feel?
- Brainstorm and come up with as many examples as possible to describe ways a pastor may keep watch over and care for you spiritually.
- Why is it important for us to know that our pastors will one day "give an account" to God for the way they cared for His people? Why do you think it was important for Scripture to include this fact?

9. How to Love Your Pastor

Now that we understand the why of supporting our pastors, we need to get practical about the how. How can you contribute to the joy of pastoring? As someone who is a pastor to pastors, let me suggest a few supersimple ways to energize your pastor's life and ministry.

Pray for your pastor daily. The enemy of your soul wants to destroy you by destroying the spiritual water carriers in your life. To cripple you and your church, the devil will try to distract and defeat your pastor by attacking everything that is important to them. Their family, their mind, their body, their children, their spouse, their personal finances, and just about every area of their lives will face the heat. Remember Jesus warned us of this saying, *the thief comes only to steal and kill and destroy* (John 10:10 NIV) and *strike the shepherd, and the sheep of the flock will be scattered* (Matthew 26:31 NIV).

Honor your pastor. Model appreciation for the job your pastor does and their willingness to expose themselves to intense heat. A mean minority may tell you that honoring pastors is not healthy in this day of equality. The Bible clearly contradicts this convenient omission because it fails to recognize the difference between strategic importance and intrinsic value. It also turns its back on the clear commands of scripture that teach us to honor our spiritual leaders.

> *The elders who direct the affairs of the church well are worthy of double honor, especially those whose work is preaching and teaching* (1 Timothy 5:17 NIV).

Have confidence in your leaders and submit to their authority, because they keep watch over you as those who must give an account. Do this so that their work will be a joy, not a burden, for that would be of no benefit to you (Hebrews 13:17 NIV).

Acknowledge those who work hard among you, who care for you in the Lord and who admonish you. Hold them in the highest regard in love because of their work. Live in peace with each other (1 Thessalonians 5:12-13 NIV).

Encourage your pastor. Most pastoral discouragement occurs because the majority tolerates an abusive minority. Instead of allowing a few "faultfinders" to establish a culture of criticism, make it a point to recognize your pastor's positive contribution to the Kingdom. Make no mistake about it, pastors are imperfect people. They have flaws, make mistakes and are by no means perfect. However, if their mistakes are discussed more than their wins are celebrated, you are contributing to a culture of discontent rather than to a culture of honor.

Give your pastor rest. Earlier I used the Space Shuttle to illustrate a spiritual truth. Let me take that illustration for a spin again. Did you know that even after landing, it takes several hours for the black tiles on the Space Shuttle to cool down? The same thing is true spiritually for your pastor. After serving under extreme spiritual heat, they must slow down, rest, and decompress. We all usually agree with this. The problem occurs when individual believers think their situation is a unique exception that warrants collapsing the margin around the pastor's time and personal life. There are a few ways you can help prevent that from happening.

- Just because you have your pastor's cell number is not a good enough reason to use it. Use restraint and give them margin.

- Be generous in giving them vacation time that is uninterrupted, timely and refreshing.
- Bless them with "rest without guilt" by not interrupting them or asking for a response on their day off.
- Instead of stopping them on Sunday morning to make a verbal request, make a phone appointment or send a detailed email explaining what you need.

Help them heal. NASA knows that some missions are so taxing upon the Shuttle that operations must be put on pause while tiles are repaired in orbit. In the same way, there will be times when your pastor faces significant discouragement, loss, humiliation, death in the family, and even extremely hurtful attacks from immature Christians. When that happens, be proactive and patient in determining how much time and resources will be required to help them heal.

Rhonda and I were blessed to have a board that understood and practiced situational awareness. After a very long and difficult building program, they gave us a nine-week sabbatical to rest and adjust to a new season of growth and expansion. When our son Geno, the church's youth pastor, was diagnosed with cancer, we went through a grueling seven-month battle for his life. I worked from my laptop in his hospital room for seven months. As you can imagine, I was exhausted and torn between my insistence to be at his side and a church that needed my leadership. The entire board assembled at my home to pray over us. Before they left, the vice-chairman spoke on behalf of the entire board and said, "Pastor, you have never let us down. We don't care if you're in the office or not. Just preach on Sundays and leave the rest to us." After Geno's death, it took me several months to find my way out of the fog, but my board knew their pastor needed time to heal and stepped up in many ways to help. As strange as it may sound, the church grew during that time as well. I attribute that growth to a loving and caring church that gave their shepherd time and margin to heal.

Be reasonable. Your pastor has a personal life that requires time, regular attention, and maintenance. Remember, they are people too! They need margin to deal with their own personal responsibilities such as paying bills, caring for their home, spending time with their family, yard work, and personal research on things like retirement planning, bidding insurance rates, and personal planning. They have parents or children that may need special care just like the rest of the population. If your high expectations cause them to neglect their personal life and burn the candle at both ends, no one wins.

If you remember anything from this chapter, I pray you will remember that like the tiles on the Space Shuttle, your pastor takes more heat than you can possibly imagine. That does not mean they are more important or valuable than you; but as NASA knows, their strategic importance to the mission requires special care in the allocation of resources. If you would like to read more about the unique pressures and struggles those in ministry face, I would recommend the book, *Pastors are People Too*, by Jimmy Dodd or my own book entitled *Isolation in Ministry: Understanding the cause, consequence and cure for a modern epidemic.* They are both available on Amazon.

Making It Real

Following are a few questions to discuss or reflect upon:
- How might your church provide a year-round prayer covering for your new pastor and family? Would you consider volunteering to head up this effort?

- How might church members fulfill the biblical mandate to honor their pastor? What might threaten a culture of honor, and what can be done to sustain it?
- Most everyone wants their pastor to have rest; but at the same time, some can unknowingly see their own needs as an exception to that rule. What are ways a church can create margin for the pastor to get rest?
- A recent study entitled "Isolation in Ministry" which can be accessed at www.agspe.org/isolation.pdf found that pastors are facing discouragement and even depression at increasingly alarming rates as God's people are becoming almost impossible to please. What do you think is contributing to this crisis of impossible expectations?
- Do you think most church people have reasonable expectations of what a pastor should be, do, and say? If so, why? If not, explain.
- As you look over the list of ways to encourage your pastor, which ones seem to be most lacking in your church?

10. Benefits of Supporting Your Pastor

The Bible teaches us that there are benefits to caring for the pastor God sends your church: *Have confidence in your leaders and submit to their authority, because they keep watch over you as those who must give an account. Do this so that their work will be a joy, not a burden, for that would be of no benefit to you* (Hebrews 13:17 NIV). If making the pastorate a burden does NOT benefit us, what does making it a joy bring to your life? Allow me to mention three things.

Your church will grow. I currently serve as the District Superintendent of the Rocky Mountain Ministry Network giving leadership to nearly 170 churches and 600 ministers serving 44,000 constituents. My role gives me a very unique perspective of the church. One of those observations is the difference between growing churches and declining churches. I have yet to see one church that has a competitive relationship with their pastor growing. Churches whose leadership community maintains a critical eye, controlling spirit, or iron grip on their pastors just do not grow. However, I have also noticed that churches that have managed to create a culture of honor, appreciation, and support have a unique momentum and growth trajectory. When you support your pastor, the church grows, budgets are met, volunteers are motivated, and pastors are more positive, energetic, and driven. I see the big picture of the "benefit" to joy that Hebrews 13:17 is talking about every week. Believe me, it is worth it.

You will be shepherded. Hebrews 13:17 teaches us that competing with your pastor is of no advantage to you, but the opposite is true. When you support, honor, and encourage your pastor, it comes back as a blessing to you, your family and even the community surrounding your church. When you support your pastor, you are better positioned for spiritual growth, maturity, community impact, and adventure.

Your pastor will be energized. To get a sneak peek of what a supported pastor looks like just image what the opposite of the words used in this verse imply. For example, when describing the consequences of having a competitive relationship with your pastor, different Bible translations of Hebrews 13:17 employ words like "burden," "no benefit," "grief," "unprofitable," "groaning," "sighing," "hard," "sadness," "sorrowful," "suffering," "drudgery," "hard," and "regretful." Who wants that? But there is good news. That means when you do not have a competitive relationship with your pastor, you can expect the opposite! You can expect your pastor and their ministry to be filled with gladness, joy, happiness, and gratefulness. It will also be beneficial, profitable, helpful, advantageous, and rewarding. It's a no-brainer!

I have been doing this thing called ministry for over 35 years. I have been an associate and lead pastor in churches small and large. I have served in two district offices and pastored pastors in the trenches of ministry. In all that time, I have yet to see one pastor suffering from an overdose of encouragement. Not one has complained of carrying the burden of love, support, or affirmation. However, what I have seen is a lot of tired, weary, overworked, and overcriticized ministers suffering under the weight of impossible expectations. However, you can help change that by deciding now to be a well of life-giving support for your new pastor.

I have also noticed that every impactful leader in the Bible had people who loyally supported them despite their weaknesses and flaws. Nehemiah had volunteers who helped him rebuild Jerusalem's wall. A few of them willingly did double duty. A small team of temple guards volunteered to work a second shift on their day off to protect their king in a vulnerable time (2 Kings 11). Abraham had 318 highly trained men who liberated his family from captivity (Genesis 14:14). In the early days of Saul's leadership, he had *valiant men, whose hearts God had touched* (1 Samuel 10:26 NIV). 2 Samuel 23 and 1 Chronicles 10 list an entire roster of men who boldly and courageously served David's vision. They are referred to as "David's mighty men" and it was said that their *faces were like the faces of lions* (1 Chronicles 12:8 ESV). Hushai was also an amazing support to David and is referred to in the Bible as *the king's friend* (1 Chronicles 27:33 ESV). Do you see the pattern? Imperfect leaders can do great things when they are supported by loyal people.

You can be that for your new pastor as well. You may not know who they are yet or where they are coming from, but that is okay. God does. The most important thing you can do right now is to decide you are going to be among those who support, love, and care for God's gift to you which the Bible calls pastor.

Making It Real

Read each of the different translations of Hebrews 13:17 below and reflect upon the questions that follow.

> *Have confidence in your leaders and submit to their authority, because they keep watch over you as those who must give an account.* <u>*Do this so that their work will be a joy, not a burden, for that would be of no benefit to you*</u> (NIV, Emphasis added).

> *Obey your leaders and submit to them, for they are keeping watch over your souls, as those who will have to give an account.* <u>*Let them do this with joy and not with groaning, for that would be of no advantage to you*</u> (ESV, Emphasis added).

Listen to your leaders and submit to their authority over the community, for they are on constant watch to protect your souls and someday they must give account. <u>Give them reason to be joyful and not to regret their duty, for that will be of no good to you</u> (VOICE, Emphasis added).

Be responsive to your pastoral leaders. Listen to their counsel. They are alert to the condition of your lives and work under the strict supervision of God. <u>Contribute to the joy of their leadership, not its drudgery. Why would you want to make things harder for them?</u> (MSG, Emphasis added).

- Read each of the four different translations above while underlining the positive words and circling the negative words. What observations do these comparisons reveal to you?
- Each of these translations attempts to communicate the meaning of the Bible's original language. Look at them closely and identify which elements of biblical truth each translation is attempting to reinforce.
- What is your own "aha moment" after looking at this verse in several different English translations?

11. Embracing God's New Thing

Earlier I addressed the importance of realizing that this pastoral transition is about your spiritual growth and focused on a few practical things you can do to grow through this season. We also looked at what the Bible has to say about honoring and supporting the spiritual water carriers in our lives and a few practical ways to do that. In this chapter, I want to address how you can embrace the new thing that God is already doing in your life and church.

Perhaps revisiting a season referred to in the Bible as a "new thing" may give us a good perspective. In the Old Testament, Israel's spiritual rebellion carried them far outside the umbrella of God's favor and protection. Times had changed, and Israel was no longer a big fish in a small pond. The northern part of the kingdom had long since backslidden and been defeated by the Assyrians. The southern kingdom followed the same path and was carried off into Babylonian captivity. As God's people suffered in the shadow of captivity, they began to think nostalgically about the past. They longed for the days when God miraculously split the Red Sea and delivered them from the Egyptians. During their nostalgia and regret, God gave the prophet Isaiah a word of hope and anticipation. He told them that their longing for the past was blinding them from the new thing God was already doing in their present. *See, I am doing a new thing! Now it springs up; do you not perceive it? I am making a way in the wilderness and streams in the wasteland* (Isaiah 43:19 NIV).

God told them that the change He was bringing to their lives was a new, current, different, and powerful thing. However, in order to benefit from it, they would need to "perceive" it.

Although your church may not be able to identify with the context of spiritual backsliding in this passage, I do think the same thing can be said about the new thing God is doing through your pastoral transition. I think embracing God's new thing still requires us to perceive and discern what God is doing and how we must respond.

Making It Real

Following are a few questions to discuss or reflect upon:

- If God loves us, why do you think He allows change to upset the routines and patterns of our lives?
- What is the difference between accepting that change is inevitable and embracing change?

12. Understanding Pastoral Etiquette

People experience different emotions when their pastor departs. Some people may feel abandoned or let down by a departing pastor. Others sometimes get their feelings hurt when a pastor leaves and no longer calls, visits, or communicates with them. Does the fact that your pastor is leaving mean they have stopped loving you? No, it does not. Something important is going on that you must understand. Your previous pastor may always be your friend, but they will not always be your pastor.

Every profession has its unique standards of ethics and etiquette, and the ministerial community is no different. They have standards and professional courtesies that are based on ethics, scripture, or common sense. There are three things that determine a pastor's theology of departure. Let's address those so you can better understand the importance of bonding with your new pastor.

God's Word. The Bible commands ministers to respect the boundaries, seasons, and calling of other pastors and ministries. The Apostle Paul modeled a deep respect for the ministry boundaries and work of fellow ministers: *It has always been my ambition to preach the gospel where Christ was not known, so that I would not be building on someone else's foundation* (Romans 15:20 NIV). When speaking of the different ministers that served in Corinth, he also said, *What, after all, is Apollos? And what is Paul? Only servants, through whom you came to believe—as the Lord has assigned to each his task* (1 Corinthians 3:5 NIV). In other words, if God calls a person away from a ministry and appoints another person to steward that work, departing ministers must recognize that their old ministry is not theirs to interfere with, build upon, or complicate. They must give themselves fully to their new ministry and leave their old assignment in the hands of a new shepherd. This is the principle that is modeled in the Bible.

Ministerial ethics. Most ministers are credentialed with a reputable denomination or credentialing authority and are accountable to them for doctrine, lifestyle, and ministerial ethics. As a minister, I happen to be credentialed with the Assemblies of God. To maintain good standing, I must renew that credential each year and sign a document agreeing to their doctrinal statement, organizational policies, and ministerial ethics. This includes my agreeing not to interfere in another pastor's ministry or communicate in a way that might undermine the credibility or influence of their new pastor. I agree not to fundraise or make requests or suggestions through anyone other than the new pastor. To do otherwise is called "discourteous conduct," and such infractions can result in my credential being placed under investigation or revoked. Why? Because my history and influence in a prior ministry does not give me the right to interfere after I have departed. God has called a new person to lead that church, and I am obligated to respect their calling and ministerial boundaries as it is the ethical thing to do.

Common sense. Ministerial ethics, etiquette, and courtesy are also based on common sense. Leadership is not a position, a title, or even an address. Leadership is influence and pastors are responsible for how they use that influence after they depart. That is why, whether it is being a doctor, a lawyer, or even an insurance agent, every profession has its own standards of professional courtesy. It is also why ministers usually make a clean break and give the new pastor margin to bond with their new congregation and develop the needed influence to lead the church into the future. John the Baptist modeled this kind of integrity and ministerial courtesy when he told his own disciples about Jesus: *He must increase, but I must decrease* (John 3:30 ESV). So if you feel this happening, do not get your feelings hurt or take it personally. Your previous pastor is just being true to their commitment to ministerial ethics and loving you enough to allow you to bond with God's new leader and your new pastor.

Making It Real

Following are a few questions to discuss or reflect upon:

- What kind of professional courtesies or ethical standards does your profession embrace or require?
- Read John 3:22-30. Why did John the Baptist tell his disciples, *He must increase, but I decrease* (v.30 ESV)?

13. *You Must Own Your Choice*

Embracing God's new thing will also require you and your church to own your choice. We are all familiar with Galatians 6:2: *Carry each other's burdens, and in this way you will fulfill the law of Christ* (NIV). It is often quoted in the context of helping others, but we sometimes ignore the statement three verses later which reads: *Each one should carry their own load* (Galatians 6:5 NIV). In other words, there are some responsibilities in life that others cannot and should not accept for us. We are the only ones who can own those duties. Your family cannot; your best friend cannot; and even your church cannot. The same principle can be applied to electing a new pastor. You will need to own your governance, attitude, and God's will.

Take responsibility for your governance. If your church is like most, you have chosen a form of governance, bylaws, or structure that allows church members to elect a pastor by some form of vote. At some point, the members of your church will cast a vote and elect a candidate that your board or search committee believes to be the most qualified, available, and willing person to lead your congregation. When you became a member or decided to attend your church, you accepted that system of confirming God's will. When that occurs, and you later disagree with something your new pastor does do not say, "I didn't vote for them" or "They're not my pastor!" Whether your vote was a yes or a no, the result of the election is decided. After the vote, your church becomes one, the person elected becomes your pastor, and you must accept the decision of the majority. Now is the time to own your decision to accept the result as God's will.

Take responsibility for your attitude. After the vote, the vote no longer counts, but your attitude does. Consequently, decide now that it is going to be cooperative, positive, and Christ-like. No one can do that for you. That is your job. Others may not be able to know if your opinion is right, but they will certainly be capable of knowing if your attitude is.

Take responsibility for God's will. When the Corinthians were divided during their own leadership transitions, Paul reminded them that it was God who assigned their leaders: *What, after all, is Apollos? And what is Paul? Only servants, through whom you came to believe—as the Lord has assigned to each his task* (1 Corinthians 3:5 NIV). Just like the Corinthians, you will need to believe that God is in this process; and if He was in it from the beginning, He is also in it in the middle and at the end. God is the one who has assigned your pastor; the vote only confirmed His will.

In many ways, choosing a pastor is a lot like a marriage. You must acknowledge the fact that you cannot love people in slices. You must accept people as they are . . . the good and the bad together. If you are married, chances are you already did this in your wedding vows. Just like marriage vows are not multiple choice, so also is choosing a pastor. Can you imagine how unreasonable and awkward it would be if your spouse thought their wedding vows were multiple-choice questions? Imagine the pastor asking your spouse to love you for better and for worse, and they yelled out, "Better! I choose better!" Or when the pastor asks if they will love you in sickness and in health, and your spouse said, "Health, I definitely choose health!" It would certainly be a strange wedding and an even more disastrous marriage. In the same way you have already accepted a form of church governance that considers the decision of your members as final confirmation of God's will. You will need to own that decision if you are going to embrace God's new thing.

Making It Real

Following are a few questions to discuss or reflect upon:

- Most churches have some sort of a system whereby a pastor is elected through the vote of the church's official members. What are negative and unhealthy ways a member may not accept or be willing to support the will of the members?
- What are positive and healthy ways a member may accept the will of the members?
- After your members vote, the vote does not matter as much as the attitude. What are some practical ways you can be proactive in having a good attitude about the result of the vote?
- Why is accepting the results of the selection process as God's will important for us as a people of faith?

14. Give Your Pastor Time

The Bible encourages situational patience: *There is a time for everything, and a season for every activity under the heavens* (Ecclesiastes 3:1 NIV). This verse is all about the convergence of timing, patience, and wisdom. The same convergence will be needed if your church is to have a successful pastoral transition.

Getting a new pastor is a lot like a heart transplant. At first the body sees the heart as a foreign object and may reject it. It takes time for the body to adjust to the heart and for the heart to adjust to the body. One of the biggest mistakes churches make is expecting too much too soon. That is why you will need to give your pastor time to learn the church, the board, the community, and the culture where all these things intersect. It is common for 90 percent of churches going through a pastoral change to experience a dip in attendance, volunteerism, and giving. It usually takes a year or two for the new pastor to regain those normal losses. Expecting your new pastor to conquer the world, please everyone, and bring explosive growth the first couple of years is unreasonable. It is as irrational as making someone run a marathon two weeks after a heart transplant. So, what are the most important areas that will require time and patience? Allow me to mention a few.

Give them time to get to know you. Please do not walk up to your new pastor during their first few months and say, "I bet you don't remember my name!" Of course, they do not. You only had to remember one or two names associated with their family, but they potentially must learn hundreds of names. In order to help your new pastor get to know you, every time you see them, stick out your hand, tell them your first and last name, and then add something unique and interesting about yourself to help them remember you. For example, I love wilderness camping and enjoy the challenge of strategic planning and being totally off grid and on my own. I have a 70-gallon water tank under the camper shell in my truck so I can haul clean water into the wilderness. I could leverage that unique quality and introduce myself in a memorable way sounding something like this:

"Hello, Pastor. My name is Gene Roncone, and I've been in the church for five years. I love camping off the grid and am the weirdo who has a 70-gallon water tank in the back of his truck. How did your second week in town go?"

You are probably wondering how often you should do this. Do it every time you see your pastor until they say your name on their own. It will take time, so do not force it and be gracious in the process.

Give them time to make changes. I am not a prophet, but I am going to go out on a limb and make a bold prediction! Your new pastor is going to run things differently than your previous pastor. Why? Because they are different. Do not make the mistake Israel made when they tried to force David to fight Goliath with Saul's armor. David's skill set was different, and his area of expertise was with a slingshot, not hand-to-hand combat. David won the battle because he was allowed to flow in his own gifting rather than his predecessor's so give them time to figure all that stuff out. Give them time to learn the church, make changes, and discover their own stride. As a matter of fact, do not criticize them for the first year. I can promise you they are going to make mistakes. I am pretty sure they are going to be imperfect so do something radical and go on a criticism fast! I am serious. Instead of criticizing and celebrating imperfection, pray for them and become part of the solution. There are no perfect people in this world which means we are going to have to learn to live with imperfection until we get to heaven.

Give them time to determine vision. The average pastorate in America today is about six and a half years. However, most growing churches are led by long-term pastors who say it was in their seventh year that they began to get traction. Leading and growing a church is not a 100-yard dash; it is a marathon. Any candidate who tells you they know what your church needs and already has a vision is probably being more optimistic than they should. Before serving in my current ministry, I pastored a thriving church for 17 years, but it was between year seven or eight that I was finally able to make good systemic decisions. It took that long to get to know the community and culture well enough to create the kind of church that was matched with what the community needed and growing to the point of requiring a new campus. Fast success is not always sustainable and can disappear as quickly as it arrived so give your pastor the time they need to win in the long haul.

Making It Real

Following are a few questions to discuss or reflect upon:
- Because your new pastor will be different and do things differently than your previous pastor, change will be unavoidable. What are some expectations you will need to be flexible with during this transition? Write them down and pray about them.
- Have you ever gone on a criticism fast? Would you be willing to find one other person in your church to do one with you and hold each other accountable? If so, who would be a good partner for you?

15. Situational Sensitivity

The Bible teaches us to be sensitive to the unique needs of others: *Let us consider how we may spur one another on toward love and good deeds, not giving up meeting together, as some are in the habit of doing, but encouraging one another—and all the more as you see the Day approaching* (Hebrews 10:24-25 NIV).

Sometimes God's people think those verses call them to encourage everyone except their pastor, but pastors need support as well. As a matter of fact, there are three areas in which a little encouragement can go a long way.

Encourage them with your words. One of the disappointing things about ministry is that pastors receive some form of negative or constructive feedback eight times for every two encouraging interactions. One reason for that is we live in an activist culture that does not know how to register criticism constructively. Another is that it is more convenient for God's people to pull the pastor aside on Sunday rather than making a phone appointment and recognizing the importance of time and place. Try to remember that Sunday is game day for your pastor. They are focused on leading a meaningful worship service, preaching an anointed sermon, and getting in the zone to hear the Spirit's voice. Recognize that, give them some margin on Sunday and use that day as an opportunity to encourage them. If they lead, preach, plan, or represent the church well, tell them. If their sermon spoke to you in a specific way, encourage them to keep listening to God. Proverbs 18:21 tells us: *The tongue has the power of life and death* (NIV). Use yours to build up your pastor rather than weakening their spirit.

Be sensitive to the unique season they are navigating. For you, Sundays will probably be the only thing that is different after your new pastor arrives. For them, change will invade every day and part of their lives. They will have a new town, address, community, and job. They will have to lean upon a new support team, neighbors, and board. If they have children, they will be attending a new school with new teachers and new friends. Financially, they will have a new checking account, pin number, passwords, address, and billing statements. They will need to find new doctors, plumbers, tax preparers, and handymen. They will be saying goodbye to people they learned to trust and be forced to depend upon strangers as they build a new support system. Pastors know what the call of God involves and do not want your sympathy, but they do need your sensitivity as change will invade EVERY area of their lives.

Pray for them. When the Amalekites attacked the Israelites at Rephidim, Moses told Joshua to fight in the valley while he prayed on the mountain.

> *[10] So Joshua fought the Amalekites as Moses had ordered, and Moses, Aaron and Hur went to the top of the hill. [11] As long as Moses held up his hands, the Israelites were winning, but whenever he lowered his hands, the Amalekites were winning. [12] When Moses' hands grew tired, they took a stone and put it under him and he sat on it. Aaron and Hur held his hands up—one on one side, one on the other—so that his hands remained steady till sunset. [13] So Joshua overcame the Amalekite army with the sword* (Exodus 17:10-13 NIV).

In very much the same way, your pastor is battling for you in the valley. The Amalekites of ministry demands, satanic attacks, and a job without boundaries can make their arms weary; but prayer is what holds them up.

Remember what the Lord said about the new thing He was doing. It was already starting and so is yours. Embrace it by being sensitive and praying for your pastor.

Making It Real

What are practical ways you can encourage your new pastor with:

- Your words?
- Your actions?
- Your prayers?
- Your thoughts?

16. Praying Your Church Through

Next to the Spirit's divine leading, prayer is the most important resource for a successful pastoral transition. The prophet Samuel not only understood the importance of prayer during leadership transitions but also perceived a lack of prayer to be sin. That is why in his farewell speech to the nation, he said: *As for me, far be it from me that I should sin against the LORD by failing to pray for you* (1 Samuel 12:23 NIV). Prayer is the one thing God expects you to bring to the table—not just you but the entire church as well!

Prayer is often presumed to be occurring during a pastoral search; however, one common mistake churches make is failing to bathe the entire process—from beginning to end—in prayer. Research by Jason Lowe of those directly involved in pastoral search committees found that prayer throughout the entire process was ranked as the number one priority, best practice, and the reason for success among effective search committees. Respondents who were dissatisfied with the result of their search process identified the lack of prayer as one of the primary reasons for their failure.[4] Jesus provided the best example that the role of prayer should have in the selection of spiritual leaders. We are told in Luke 6:12-15 that Jesus prayed all night the day before He selected the apostles. Acts 14:21-25 also shows us that the early church prayed and fasted before appointing local pastors.

During my extensive research on pastoral transitions, nearly every resource I read mentioned the importance of prayer. However, I only recall one that provided practical examples and resources on how to apply prayer to the pastoral selection process.[5] Author Chris Brauns laments this fatal omission: *Most pastoral search committees struggle with a presumption of self-sufficiency . . . The biggest clue to self-reliance felt by pastoral search committees is the small amount of attention they devote to prayer.*[6]

Intentional prayer will require a specific strategy. That is why I invested a considerable amount of time thinking through this topic and creating a prayer guide that covers every stage and person involved in a pastoral transition. This prayer guide can be rotated every forty days until the end of your pastoral search. I would recommend using it to mobilize the entire church behind one practical thing to pray about each day.[7]

Feel free to use the PDF version that can be downloaded at www.agspe.org/Rise_Up_Prayer.pdf and made available to your people on Sundays. The PDF version also includes a hyperlink to a short podcast outlining six positive things your people can do to support the board during the pastoral transition.

RISE UP — 40 DAYS OF PRAYER
Pastoral Search Prayer Focus

Knowing that the most underutilized source of spiritual power in ministry is the intercession for Christian leaders, we would like to call the church to pray for one of the following focuses each day of the month during this transition. Continue rotating through the list until our new pastor arrives.

1. **FAMILY DURING TRANSITION:** Pray for our future pastor's family during the transition that they would experience a smooth changeover and discover their place of ministry.
2. **STRENGTH FOR TRANSITION:** Pray for our future pastor to have strength to endure the changes of

transition (relocation, selling/buying a home, moving, packing/unpacking).

3. **UNITY:** Pray for our church to be united during the pastoral transition.

4. **TRANSITIONAL LEADERSHIP:** Pray for our board, staff, interim pastor, and guest speakers during this transition.

5. **CHARACTER:** Pray for all those involved on both sides of the transition process to have integrity, honesty, and trust in God.

6. **COURAGE:** Pray for our Board to have the courage to make decisions; take unfavorable positions, if necessary; uphold standards; and act decisively without fear.

7. **DISCERNMENT:** Pray for our Board and future pastor to have wisdom to ask the right questions and discern between better and best.

8. **AFFECTED MINISTERS:** Pray for the staff ministers and their families on both sides of this transition. Pray that God would give them faith, trust, and the ability to bless their respective churches in this transition.

9. **AGREEMENT:** Pray for the Board to be in agreement regarding the background and experience needed by the next pastor.

10. **SENSITIVITY TO NEEDS:** Pray for the Board to place the church's needs before their own as they read applications, listen to sermons, and talk with candidates.

11. **SITUATIONAL WISDOM:** Pray for our future pastor to have the ability to address critical needs and make wise decisions in a short period of time.

12. **DISCERNMENT:** Pray for the Board to be led by God's Spirit and know the right questions to ask as they represent the church in the interview process.

13. **FAITH AND OPTIMISM:** Pray for our church to have unusual faith, patience, and trust that God is leading and guiding this process.

14. **JUDGMENT:** Pray for the Board to have clarity as they interview, eliminate, and move forward with candidates in the interview process.
15. **HONESTY:** Pray for the Board to represent the church accurately, truthfully, and attractively.
16. **TEAM CHEMISTRY:** Pray for our future pastor to have the ability to quickly find, appoint, and delegate tasks to the right people.
17. **WISDOM TO NETWORK:** Pray for those outside the church who will be assisting the Board to be sensitive to and led by the Holy Spirit.
18. **RESOURCES:** Pray for our people to remain faithful in their tithes, offerings, and missions giving during the pastoral transition. Also pray that God will lead and enable others to give to the transition fund so that our new pastor has resources to implement vision.
19. **SURRENDER:** Pray for those with influence in the search process to subordinate their personal agendas to what is best for the church.
20. **PHYSICAL STAMINA:** Pray for our Board to have physical endurance to handle all the necessary demands of this process.
21. **DISCERNMENT:** Pray for our Board to have discernment in sorting through all the various styles, philosophies, and ministry models represented by pastoral candidates.
22. **AFFECTED MINISTRY:** Pray for the church or ministry that our future pastor will be leaving. Pray for them to have faith, wisdom, and divine leading in their own transition.
23. **PATIENCE:** Pray for our church to have the ability to trust God and others while investing the necessary time and resources in the pastoral search.
24. **REASONABLE EXPECTATIONS:** Pray for the Board not to settle for too little or aim too high thereby setting unreasonable or unattainable expectations.

25. **SPIRIT-FILLED LIFE:** Pray for our Board and future pastor to be led by and walk in the Spirit.

26. **DEPARTING MINISTRY:** Pray for the ministry our future pastor will be transitioning out of to assume new leadership. Pray for their previous church's search committee to have a healthy transition and for their denominational executives to be led by the Lord to assist them.

27. **TEAM CHEMISTRY:** Pray for our future pastor to have deacons, staff, and employees who genuinely support their ministry values, philosophy, and initiatives.

28. **PEACE:** Pray for the candidate and the candidate's family to have clarity during their visits with the church and know whether this is the next step of ministry to which God is calling them.

29. **WISDOM IN EVALUATING NEEDS:** Pray for our Board and interim pastor to have discernment in evaluating the needs and opportunities in this transition.

30. **AFFECTED FAMILIES:** Pray for the ministry staff and family members on both sides of this transition who will need to adjust, support, and serve with a new leader.

31. **FORWARD VISION:** Pray for our future pastor to receive a divine burden and direction as well as outreach to our community and city.

32. **DIVINE CALL:** Pray for our future pastor to sense an irresistible call and mandate from God to lead this church.

33. **SEARCH COMMITTEE:** Pray for the future search committee in the ministry our future pastor will leave. Pray for them to have wisdom, faith, and clarity in their own search.

34. **ROLE CLARIFICATION:** Pray for the Board to have clarity as to the characteristics, goals, and responsibilities that should be included in the position description for the next pastor.

35. **MULTIGENERATIONAL:** Pray for our future pastor to be able to relate to the various generations and cultures represented in our church.
36. **SUSTAINABILITY:** Pray for our church not to experience declines in attendance, giving, volunteerism, and morale during this pastoral transition.
37. **PROTECTION:** Pray for no individuals to choose to use this leadership vacuum as a time to promote their own agenda and preferences. Pray for the church to be protected from selfish ambition and that those attempting to do so will be lovingly corrected by the Holy Spirit.
38. **SENSITIVITY:** Pray for the Board to hear God's voice with clarity and have peace concerning who should be interviewed.
39. **OPTIMISTIC ANTICIPATION:** Pray for the future pastor, spouse, and family to feel the same peace and excitement that the Board feels about them.
40. **MUTUAL CONFIRMATION:** Pray for the entire congregation to feel a sense of peace and confirmation as the new pastor is confirmed through the vote of the official membership.

Few things can help your church overcome obstacles, find God's will, and be led by the Spirit than prayer so why not decide now to make it a priority for you and your church throughout the entire transition.

17. Financing the Future

America is known throughout the world as a superpower, but it has not always been that way. During the War of Independence, the nation almost died several times because it could not finance the revolution. Had it not been for Haym Salomon, America would have perished in its infancy. Salomon was a successful merchant, financier, and one of George Washington's personal friends. When the fledgling nation ran out of food, munitions, and supplies, his generosity often prevailed. As an immigrant, he saw hope and promise in the American dream. Records reveal Salomon's fundraising and personal lending helped provide over $650,000 to finance the war. That is approximately $16 million in 2022 dollars. His face is not carved into Mount Rushmore, but his vision of the future has made the realities of our present possible.

Salomon gave because he was able to look beyond what was and remain committed to a vision of what could be. Every vision needs a Washington to dream and a Salomon to fund. I think the same thing can be said about great churches. That is why you should pray about making a generous donation, above your normal tithes and offerings, to help your church establish a transition fund.

A common misconception about pastoral transitions is that the church will save money because they will not have to pay a pastor's salary. Searching for a pastor is a significant expense worthy of the benefits it brings. Cutting corners only results in depriving your church of the steps, coaching and resources needed to make wise decisions and identify God's will. The Bible encourages us to be as strategic with our budgeting as we are with our process:

²⁸For which of you, desiring to build a tower, does not first sit down and count the cost, whether he has enough to complete it? ²⁹Otherwise, when he has laid a foundation and is not able to finish, all who see it begin to mock him, ³⁰saying, "This man began to build and was not able to finish" (Luke 14:28-30, ESV).

Most churches experiencing a pastoral transition will end up spending more, not less, even though they will have a short break from paying a lead pastor's salary. When anticipating expenses, it is important to distinguish between hidden and hard costs. Hidden costs are expenses indirectly related to the transition while hard costs include expenses directly related to the search process. A transition fund will help your church absorb both and transform obligation into opportunity.

Hidden costs. Many churches fail to consider the indirect costs of a pastoral transition. Authors Carolyn Weese and J. Russell Crabtree dedicated an entire chapter of their book to warning church boards of the significant financial impact of a pastoral search. As consultants specializing in pastoral transitions, they listed some of the following considerations among their list of hidden costs:[8]

- **Attendance.** Churches in transition often experience a 10-15 percent decrease in attendance that will take the new pastor one to two years to regain.
- **Income.** It is also common for churches in transition to experience a 10-15 percent decrease in tithes and offerings that will also take one to two years to recuperate.
- **New members.** Within the first six months of a pastoral transition, churches experience a 50 percent decrease in new members and families deciding to associate with the church.

- **Salaries.** Most churches experiencing a pastoral transition (especially those whose pastor served ten years or more) find their current salary is around ten percent lower than the industry norm and will need to be increased to appeal to competent candidates.
- **Staff adjustments.** If your church has other paid staff, you may also have some turnover before and after the placement of a new pastor. This is normal.

Hard costs. Because transitions are inevitable, expenses related to them are also unavoidable. These expenses will include things like:
- **Farewell expenses.** These expenses include things related to taking care of and honoring the departing pastor. Examples would include paying off unused vacation, a farewell celebration, an appreciation gift, severance pay, continuation of benefits, retirement gift or previously agreed reimbursements that have not been paid.
- **Interim expenses.** These expenses are related to the cost of keeping the church moving forward in the interim. Examples would include costs associated with a sustainability initiative, honorariums and hosting of guest speakers, updating technology, hiring temporary office help, and filling in gaps created by the pastor and their spouse's departure.
- **Search expenses.** These are expenses related to identifying and interviewing candidates. Examples would include costs like coaching and resourcing for the board, advertising the opening, and travel expenses for your screening team to visit the final candidate's church in order to experience their ministry firsthand. They also would include expenses related to interviewing potential candidates and hosting the final candidate to be voted upon and then return to secure housing.

- **Post search expenses.** These expenses are related to relocating a new pastor and assimilating them into your community and a new work environment. Examples would include moving expenses, a welcoming party, office furniture, and providing necessary computer or technology that needs updated or replaced.

Transition fund. Your transition is going to involve a combination of "best case," "likely case," and "worst case" situations. Donating above your normal giving to the transition fund will help your board hope for the best and plan for the worst. I always recommend that churches in transition try to establish a transition fund equal to one month of the church's normal income. After your new pastor arrives and all expenses have been paid, you can then make any remaining balance available to help finance the new pastor's first initiative. It is a win/win strategy.

Over the years, I have become convinced that having a transition fund is as important to this process as the Holy Spirit's direction. Proverbs 27:12 reminds us that *a prudent person foresees danger and takes precautions. The simpleton goes blindly on and suffers the consequences* (NLT).

Salomon's vision of American potential was so clear that he willingly financed the future at a time when it was needed most. You can do the same for your church.

Making It Real

Following are a few questions to discuss or reflect upon:
- What are things you can do without over the next 2-3 months that would enable you to reallocate those funds in the form of a donation to the church's transition fund?

- If you were part of the board, what kind of emotions might you feel if people started giving money to the transition fund?
- What figure would represent your best gift of faith at this time?

18. Defying Gravity

Statistics repeatedly reveal that churches in pastoral transition can experience a substantial decline in morale, attendance, and giving. Attendance and income will decrease between 10 and 15 percent. I have found that in most cases, attendance will decline about 5 to 10 percent more than giving will. This is even true of healthy churches. However, instead of just accepting the gravitational pull of transition, why not believe God to sustain or even increase morale, resources, and engagement during this time. Why not step out like Joshua and believe God to defy gravity and enable an anomaly of faith.

> *12On the day the LORD gave the Amorites over to Israel, Joshua said to the LORD in the presence of Israel: "Sun, stand still over Gibeon, and you, moon, over the Valley of Aijalon." 13So the sun stood still, and the moon stopped, till the nation avenged itself on its enemies, as it is written in the Book of Jashar. The sun stopped in the middle of the sky and delayed going down about a full day. 14There has never been a day like it before or since, a day when the LORD listened to a human being. Surely the LORD was fighting for Israel!* (Joshua 10:12-14 NIV).

Why not be a gravity defying force in your church during this pastoral transition? Why not stand tall with your church board, point your finger to the sky and say in faith, "Sun, stand still!" That is why I am asking you to make a commitment to support your church during the first year of this pastoral transition. You can do that by giving God an offering of your commitment in the following areas.

Standing Together in Unity

I agree and commit the following to God, myself, and other members of my church community:

1. **Prayer.** I will pray daily for our board, staff, volunteers, church, and future pastoral family.
2. **Trust.** I will trust God to use the search process to identify our future pastor.
3. **Faith.** I will have faith and stay optimistic and spiritually expectant.
4. **Committed.** I will sustain my commitment, faithfulness, attendance, giving, and service during the transition.
5. **Patience.** I will have fair expectations, be patient, and give our future pastor and their family the time needed to adjust to a new community, church, and work environment.
6. **United.** I will seek to build unity and resist selfishness, division, and the desire to force my preferences on others.
7. **Sensitivity.** I will be sensitive to our staff, volunteers, and workers by supporting and encouraging them during this interim time.
8. **Hope.** I will trust our deacons to be led by the Holy Spirit, sensitive to the needs of our church and community, and be unified as they seek God's will.
9. **Cooperative.** I will take responsibility for the final decision that the members make in selecting our new pastor.
10. **Support.** I will support our new pastor and seek to understand the vision and burdens the Lord will place upon their heart.

Name _____ Date _____

Why not start a chain reaction in your church by signing this commitment page, photocopying it, and giving a copy to your church board.

Making It Real

Following are a few questions to discuss or reflect upon:

- Look at the list of commitments above. Which ones come easier to you and why?
- Look at the list of commitments above. Which ones come harder for you and why?
- If you were the devil, what would you be doing to tempt and distract the church at this time?
- How might your church members who are adopting a predetermined mindset now benefit the church in one year?

Endnotes

[1] To access the entire family of Rise Up pastoral transition resources, go to www.generoncone.org/riseup.

[2] Richard Clinton, *Starting Well: Building a Strong Foundation for a Lifetime of Ministry*, Barnabas Publishers, Altadena, CA, 1994, pp. 11-13.

[3] Eric Metaxas and Roberto Rivera, "A Pastor's Suicide: An All-Too Familiar Story," *The Christian Post*, September 19, 2018, https://www.christianpost.com/voice/a-pastors-suicide-an-all-too-familiar-story.html, accessed October 17, 2018.

[4] Jason Lowe, *Searching for Ways to Search for a Pastor, An Examination of the Best & Worst Practices in the Pastor Search Process*, June 4, 2018, https://jasonalowe.com/wp-content/uploads/2018/06/pastor-search-survey-results-report.pdf, accessed on June 6, 2022.

[5] Jason Lowe, *The Church During the Search, Honoring Christ While You Wait for Your Next Pastor*, Abbotsford, WI, Aneko Press, 2020, pp. 75-98. [Chapter 4 on prayer is outstanding.]

[6] Chris Brauns, *When the Word Leads Your Pastoral Search: Biblical Principles and Practices to Guide Your Search*, Moody Publishers, Chicago, Illinois, 2011, p. 25.

[7] This prayer list was compiled by Pastor Gene Roncone from different resources over many years. Unfortunately, it would be impossible to recall their original sources.

[8] Carolyn Weese and J. Russell Crabtree, *The Elephant in the Boardroom: Speaking the Unspoken About Pastoral Transitions*, Jossey-Bass Publishers, Hoboken, NY, 2004, pp. 29-40.

Made in the USA
Middletown, DE
20 September 2022